BEN MEYERS

Mastering Anxiety for the Anxious Human

A Real-Life Guide to Tackling Worry, Finding Peace, and Owning Your Journey

Contents

1

Mastering Anxiety for the Anxious Human

A Real-Life Guide to Tackling Worry, Finding Peace, and Owning Your Journey

2

Welcome to Your Journey of Mastering Anxiety

Welcome, and thank you for taking this step toward better understanding your anxiety. Whether you're feeling overwhelmed, looking for answers, or simply ready to make a change, this book is here to support you on your journey.

In the pages ahead, you'll learn not just what anxiety is, but *how* it works in your mind and body. You'll discover practical tools and strategies that can help you calm your thoughts, soothe your body, and approach anxiety with a fresh perspective. From understanding your triggers and reframing anxious thoughts to practicing mindfulness and building self-care habits, this book is designed to give you everything you need to take back control.

By the end of this book, you can expect to:

- Gain a deeper understanding of how anxiety shows up in your life, and why.
- Feel empowered to navigate anxious thoughts and emotions

with greater ease.
- Develop a personalized toolkit of coping strategies to reduce stress, manage triggers, and find calm when you need it most.
- Build daily habits and routines that support long-term mental well-being and resilience.
- Approach anxiety with greater self-compassion, humor, and confidence, creating space for more joy and peace in your life.

The goal here isn't to eliminate anxiety entirely—because anxiety is a natural part of being human—but to help you build a healthier relationship with it, so it no longer holds you back from living the life you want. You'll walk away feeling more equipped to handle whatever comes your way, with a deeper sense of self-awareness and empowerment.

If at any point during your journey you feel the need for further support—whether through personalized coaching, consulting, or simply more resources—please know that you can find additional guidance and information on my website: www.somebodylikeyou.org. I'm here to help you deepen your understanding, strengthen your skills, and provide support as you navigate this journey.

So, take a deep breath, and let's dive in. You've got this, and I'm right here with you every step of the way.

3

What is Anxiety? – Making Sense of the Basics

Hey there! So here we are, diving into the world of anxiety. And let me say this right off the bat: if you've been feeling overwhelmed, stressed, or like your mind is running on a hamster wheel, you are definitely not alone. Understanding anxiety is a journey, and the fact that you're here means you're ready to take the first step. That's huge, and you should give yourself some credit for even opening this book.

So let's talk about anxiety—what it really is, how it works, and why it sometimes feels like your body and mind are in a never-ending game of "What could possibly go wrong?" The good news is, we're going to make sense of this together.

What Exactly is Anxiety?

Anxiety is your body's built-in way of saying, *"Hey, pay attention—something might be up!"* Think of it as that friend who always worries about *everything*, like reminding you to double-check the locks before bed or asking, *"Did you remember to bring your umbrella?"* That's anxiety in a nutshell: a helpful (but sometimes overprotective) warning system that's trying to keep you safe.

Here's the deal: anxiety evolved as part of our survival instinct. Imagine you're back in the days of early humans, walking through a dense forest, when suddenly you hear a rustling in the bushes. Now, it could be a rabbit... or a saber-toothed tiger. Your brain doesn't wait to figure out which one—it just wants to keep you alive. So, it kicks into gear, flooding your body with adrenaline and other hormones to get you ready to react, whether that means fighting, running away, or just freezing on the spot.

Fast forward to today: no more saber-toothed tigers (thank goodness), but plenty of other triggers. And the funny thing is, your brain doesn't know the difference between *"I need to run from a predator"* and *"I have a big work presentation tomorrow."* Both situations send your body into a similar state of high alert.

That's why you get that racing heart, shallow breathing, tense muscles—all part of your body gearing up to protect you. It's like your brain is saying, *"Okay, let's do this! I'm ready for anything!"* Even if all you're doing is trying to make a decision about what to eat for dinner.

Normal Anxiety vs. Anxiety Disorders

So, let's break down something important. We all feel anxiety sometimes—whether it's those pre-interview jitters, that feeling of dread when you're running late, or the way your stomach flips when you're in a social situation that feels a bit awkward. That's normal. Anxiety is part of life, and honestly, it can even be helpful. It's what motivates you to prepare, stay safe, or do your best.

But what happens when anxiety sticks around for the long haul? Or shows up uninvited to every occasion? That's when things start shifting from "normal" anxiety to what might be considered an anxiety disorder.

Here's the difference:

1. **Frequency**: Is your anxiety showing up every now and then, or is it camping out like an uninvited houseguest who won't leave?
2. **Intensity**: When anxiety does pop up, how strong is it? Mild, like a passing breeze, or intense, like a storm that makes it hard to think about anything else?
3. **Impact**: And probably the most important—how is this anxiety affecting your life? If it's keeping you from doing things you want or need to do, then it might be time to take a closer look.

So, if anxiety is occasionally nudging you to be careful or prepared, that's normal. But if it feels like it's taking over, making everyday tasks feel like climbing Mount Everest, then it's worth exploring what might be going on.

Anxiety and the Brain – Your Built-In Alarm System

Let's take a little trip inside that incredible brain of yours. When anxiety hits, it's because a part of your brain called the amygdala is waving a big red flag. The amygdala is like your brain's alarm system, and when it thinks there's a threat, it sets off a whole-body reaction to get you ready to respond.

The chain reaction goes something like this: The amygdala sends a signal to the hypothalamus, which then activates your body's "fight or flight" response. But it's not just "fight or flight." Anxiety actually has four ways of responding to perceived danger:

- **Fight**: When your anxiety shows up as aggression, anger, or defensiveness, it's like your brain is saying, *"Bring it on—I'm ready to handle this!"* That might mean snapping at someone or feeling the need to argue your point, even when it's not necessary.
- **Flight**: Ever feel like you just want to escape a situation? That's anxiety telling you to get out of dodge. It could be anything from leaving a social event early to avoiding a difficult conversation altogether.
- **Freeze**: If you've ever felt stuck, unable to act or make a decision, that's the freeze response kicking in. It's like your brain says, *"Let's just pause here until we figure out what's safe."*
- **Fawn**: And then there's the lesser-known response—fawn.

This is when your brain tells you to keep the peace and avoid conflict by doing whatever it takes to make others happy. Agreeing to do something you didn't want to just to keep someone else calm? That's "fawn."

It's all about your brain trying to figure out the best way to keep you safe. And while these responses were great for ancient humans facing real physical danger, they can be a little... let's say, inconvenient in the modern world.

Anxiety Isn't Always the Bad Guy

So here's the thing that might surprise you: anxiety isn't always your enemy. It's trying to protect you, even if it sometimes overreacts or shows up at the wrong time. Think of it like your body's smoke detector—it's there to alert you when there's smoke (or, in this case, potential danger). The problem is, sometimes it goes off when there's just burnt toast and not an actual fire.

The point is, anxiety has good intentions. It's like that over-protective friend who texts you to make sure you got home safe... and then calls you when you haven't replied within five minutes. You can appreciate its concern while also working to help it calm down when things are actually okay.

Reflect on Your Own Experience

Take a moment to think about how anxiety shows up for you. Does it show up before big events, or maybe when things are quiet, and your mind has space to wander? What are those situations that set off your alarm system—whether it's a racing heart, sweaty palms, or that general feeling of *"Oh no, what if...?"*

This isn't about judgment; it's about understanding. Start noticing when and where anxiety shows up, what it feels like, and what thoughts pop into your head. That's the first step to figuring out how to respond differently.

Key Takeaways

- **Anxiety is Part of Life**: Everyone feels it—you're not alone, and there's nothing "wrong" with you for experiencing anxiety.
- **It's Here to Help (Really!)**: Anxiety's job is to protect you, even if it sometimes gets a little too enthusiastic.
- **You Can Work with It**: Understanding your brain's "alarm system" (fight, flight, freeze, or fawn) is the first step to working with your anxiety instead of against it.

This journey is about getting to know yourself better, finding ways to manage anxiety when it pops up, and creating a healthier relationship with those feelings of stress, nervousness, or fear. You've got this, and I'm here with you every step of the way.

4

Anxiety in Disguise – The Many Faces of Anxiety

By now, you know that anxiety is like that super-sensitive bodyguard that's always on the lookout for trouble. But here's the thing—anxiety doesn't always show up looking like what you'd expect. It's kind of a master of disguise. One day, it could look like nerves before a big meeting; the next, it could show up as anger, perfectionism, or a physical ache that makes you wonder, *"Is something actually wrong with me?"* So, let's dive into all the ways anxiety might try to blend in with your everyday life, because recognizing it is the first step to understanding it.

The Chameleons of Anxiety – When Anxiety Isn't Obvious

Here's the tricky part: anxiety doesn't always make a grand entrance. It's not like you wake up every day thinking, *"Ah, yes, that's my anxiety acting up!"* Instead, it has this sneaky way of wearing different masks. And sometimes, anxiety hides behind behaviors, emotions, or even physical symptoms that seem unrelated.

Anxiety as Perfectionism

Ever feel like you have to get everything *just right*? That if one tiny detail is off, the whole world might fall apart? Anxiety loves this kind of thinking because it tricks you into believing that if you can make everything perfect, then you'll be safe. But here's the kicker—perfectionism often sets up impossible standards, so when you don't meet them, guess who shows up to remind you? Yep, anxiety.

For example, let's say you're hosting a family dinner. You've cleaned the house, cooked a three-course meal, and made sure everything is in its place. Then, right before everyone arrives, you notice a tiny stain on one of the napkins, and suddenly it feels like the whole dinner is ruined. That's anxiety disguising itself as perfectionism—setting sky-high standards and freaking out when they're not met.

Anxiety as Irritability or Anger

Have you ever found yourself snapping at someone over something small, and then later wondered why you were so quick to anger? Sometimes, anxiety hides behind irritability. It's like having all this pent-up energy and not knowing what to do with it, so it spills out in quick, defensive reactions. If you've ever had a stressful day and then found yourself getting disproportionately annoyed because someone left dishes in the sink, you're not alone.

Anxiety can make everything feel bigger than it really is, so small annoyances can seem like huge issues. And once that frustration hits, it's easy to react without realizing anxiety was driving the car.

Anxiety as Avoidance

Ah, good ol' avoidance. This one is a classic. When anxiety makes a situation feel too overwhelming to deal with, your brain's first instinct might be to avoid it entirely. It's like when you have a pile of unread emails, and instead of answering them one by one, you just pretend they don't exist. Problem solved, right? Except... not really.

Avoidance might help you feel better in the short term, but in the long term, it tends to make anxiety stronger. Because every time you avoid something that makes you anxious, you're teaching your brain that the best way to deal with fear is to run from it, which only reinforces the anxiety.

Anxiety as Physical Symptoms

This one catches a lot of people off guard. Anxiety doesn't just stay in your head; it affects your whole body. Tight muscles, headaches, stomachaches, dizziness, racing heart, or even feeling like you can't breathe—all these symptoms can be your body's way of processing anxiety. Sometimes it feels like your body is carrying the anxiety for you when your mind can't.

And let's be real, physical symptoms can be terrifying. It's easy to wonder, *"Am I sick? Is something really wrong with me?"*

But the reality is, anxiety has a way of showing up as physical sensations. Think of it like your body waving a little flag that says, *"Hey, pay attention to me—something's going on!"*

The Many Faces of Anxiety Disorders

Anxiety likes variety, and there's no one-size-fits-all way that it shows up. It's kind of like a shapeshifter, and it can look different for everyone. That's why there are so many different forms of anxiety disorders. Let's break down a few of the most common ones and how they might show up in day-to-day life.

Generalized Anxiety Disorder (GAD)

If you ever feel like your mind is a "worry machine," constantly producing thoughts about anything and everything, you might be familiar with GAD. It's like having a running list of "What ifs" that never seems to end: *"What if I mess up at work?"* *"What if I get sick?"* *"What if I forgot to turn off the stove?"* And even when you manage to solve one problem, anxiety will often find another one to latch onto.

Social Anxiety

Ever find yourself playing out an entire conversation in your head before you actually talk to someone? Social anxiety makes social situations feel like high-stakes performances. It's the fear of being judged, embarrassed, or rejected, even if there's no real reason to believe those things will happen. So, whether it's meeting new people, speaking up in a group, or even making small talk, social anxiety turns everyday interactions into situations that feel more like marathons than sprints.

Panic Disorder

This is when anxiety shows up like a tidal wave—sudden, intense, and overwhelming. Panic attacks can happen out of nowhere, and they can make you feel like you're losing control, having a heart attack, or even dying. It's an incredibly scary experience, but it's your body's "fight or flight" system going into overdrive. Panic disorder can make you start fearing the panic attacks themselves, leading to more anxiety about when the next one might happen.

Phobias

A phobia is a fear that's way out of proportion to the actual threat. Heights, spiders, flying, tight spaces—phobias are specific fears that can be so intense they lead to avoidance of certain situations. For someone with a fear of flying, even the thought of an upcoming flight might trigger anxiety, while someone with a fear of heights might start feeling anxious just looking at a photo of a tall building.

Obsessive-Compulsive Disorder (OCD)

OCD is a bit of a double whammy—obsessions (intrusive, un-wanted thoughts) and compulsions (the behaviors you feel you *have* to do to relieve those thoughts). It's like your brain latches onto something and won't let go until you perform a certain action to "fix" it. But the thing is, the relief is temporary, and the anxiety usually comes right back, making you feel like you're stuck in a loop.

A Day in the Life – Seeing Anxiety in Action

Let's paint a picture. Imagine you're getting ready for work. You wake up and immediately start thinking about your to-do list for the day—*"I have that meeting at 10 am, but I also need to respond to all those emails, and oh, I hope I don't forget to pick up groceries after work."* As you're making breakfast, you accidentally spill your coffee, and suddenly it feels like the whole morning is ruined. You start feeling tightness in your chest as you clean it up, mentally replaying the day's schedule over and over.

Later on, at work, a coworker says, *"We need to talk later,"* and that one statement sets off a whole spiral of thoughts: *"Did I do something wrong? Are they mad at me? What could they possibly want to talk about?"* By the time 3 pm rolls around, you're drained, tense, and feeling like you've been running a marathon—even though you haven't left your desk all day.

This is anxiety in action: it pops up in thoughts, shows up in your body, and affects your reactions to everyday events.

Reflecting on Your Anxiety Masks

So let's get a little introspective. How does anxiety like to "disguise" itself in your life? Does it look like over-preparing for things? Does it come up as tension in your neck and shoulders?

Or maybe it looks like procrastination, avoiding that task you've been putting off. Whatever form it takes, knowing how anxiety shows up for you is a powerful first step in taking back control.

And remember, you're not supposed to have all the answers right now. This is a journey of learning and discovery, and you're right where you need to be.

Key Takeaways

- **Anxiety is a Master of Disguise**: It doesn't always show up as obvious fear or worry—it can hide behind perfectionism, irritability, avoidance, and even physical symptoms.
- **Everyone's Anxiety Looks Different**: There are many types of anxiety disorders, each with their own patterns and triggers. Understanding your specific anxiety is key to managing it.
- **It's Okay to Be Curious About Your Anxiety**: This is about exploring how anxiety shows up for you without judgment. Knowing is half the battle, and awareness is the first step toward change.

So now that we've talked about how anxiety can disguise itself, let's keep going on this journey to learn how to recognize it, understand it, and—most importantly—work with it. You're doing great, and I'm right here with you.

5

The Science of Stress – What's Happening Inside?

Alright, now that we've talked about what anxiety is and the many forms it can take, let's get to the heart (and brain) of the matter—what's actually going on in your body when anxiety hits? I promise this won't be a boring science lesson, but understanding a bit about what's happening inside can be a total game-changer. And don't worry—I'll break it down so it makes sense, and maybe even make you chuckle a little along the way.

Stress vs. Anxiety – How Are They Related?

Let's clear up something right away: stress and anxiety are *not* the same thing, though they're close friends who like to hang out together. You could think of stress as the external pressures you experience—deadlines at work, a busy family schedule, that surprise bill that hits your mailbox on a Friday evening (because, of course, it's Friday).

Stress is the stuff happening *to* you, and it's what triggers your body's stress response. Anxiety, on the other hand, is your internal response to stress. It's what happens when that stress sticks around for a while, keeps you on high alert, and convinces your brain that even when the situation is over, it might come back again.

A helpful way to look at it: stress is like the traffic you deal with on your daily commute, and anxiety is the "what if I get stuck in traffic again tomorrow?" thoughts that pop up in your head later that night.

Your Body's Alarm System – The Fight, Flight, Freeze, or Fawn Response

Let's break this down a little further. When your brain senses danger (and remember, it's not just talking about bears or tigers—it could be anything that feels threatening to you, like social situations, uncertainty, or conflict), it triggers the "fight, flight, freeze, or fawn" response. Think of it like your brain's emergency button—it's pressed, and suddenly your whole body is on high alert.

1. **Fight**: Your body gears up to confront the situation head-on. You might feel angry, defensive, or like you're ready to take action.
2. **Flight**: Your brain wants you to get out of there as fast as possible. Heart's pounding, palms are sweaty—you're ready to run from the situation (even if it's just mentally checking out).

3. **Freeze**: Think "deer in the headlights." Your body locks up, like you're stuck, and it can be hard to make a move or a decision.
4. **Fawn**: This is all about keeping the peace. Your brain says, *"Let's just go along with whatever everyone else wants, so we don't rock the boat."*

It's like your brain is a control center, figuring out which of these responses is going to keep you safest. And to make sure you're ready for whichever response it chooses, it floods your body with adrenaline and cortisol (your stress hormones), which rev up your heart rate, speed up your breathing, and make your muscles ready for action.

Your Brain's Key Players – Amygdala, Prefrontal Cortex, and Hypothalamus

It's time to introduce the key players in your brain's anxiety response team. Don't worry—I promise not to throw a bunch of confusing science terms at you without making sense of them first. Let's meet the team:

1. The Amygdala – The Alarm System

This little almond-shaped part of your brain is basically the smoke detector. When the amygdala thinks there's something threatening going on, it raises the alarm, which sets off your fight, flight, freeze, or fawn response. It's quick to act (some-times *too* quick), and it's not interested in weighing out pros and cons—it just wants to keep you safe right now.

So, if you suddenly feel anxiety before speaking in public or walking into a crowded room, that's your amygdala doing its job. Sure, it's kind of like that overprotective friend who's always worried about something going wrong, but it means well.

2. The Prefrontal Cortex – The Rational Thinker

This is the part of your brain that thinks things through, helps you make decisions, and problem-solve. It's the voice of reason that tries to say, *"Okay, let's slow down and figure out if this is really a threat or not."* But here's the catch: your prefrontal cortex can be overridden by your amygdala when that alarm system goes off. That's why when you're anxious, it can be hard to "think straight" or talk yourself out of being worried.

In a perfect world, the prefrontal cortex and amygdala work together, balancing each other out. But when anxiety kicks in, it's often like the amygdala hogs the microphone and won't let the prefrontal cortex get a word in edgewise.

3. The Hypothalamus – The Master Controller

Once the amygdala hits the panic button, the hypothalamus is like, *"Got it! Let's get the body ready!"* It sends out all the right signals to release those stress hormones (adrenaline and cortisol), which trigger changes throughout your body. Heart rate increases, muscles tense, blood flow speeds up—it's your body getting ready to respond to the perceived danger.

The Hormone Cocktail – What's Happening in Your Body

When anxiety hits, your body goes into full action mode, and that means hormones start pumping. Let's break down what those hormones are and what they do:

1. **Adrenaline**: This is the body's "get up and go" hormone. It boosts your energy, gets your muscles ready for action, and makes you super alert. It's why you might feel that rush of energy when you're anxious—it's your body getting you ready to deal with the threat, whatever that may be.
2. **Cortisol**: This one's often called the "stress hormone." It helps manage how your body uses carbohydrates, fats, and proteins, and it gives your body the energy it needs to handle whatever's going on. But when cortisol sticks around too long (like in chronic stress situations), it can lead to all kinds of issues—sleep problems, changes in mood, digestive issues, you name it.

So when you're anxious, your body is flooded with this hormone cocktail to help you respond quickly. It's really useful when you need to react fast—like in an actual emergency—but not so much when you're sitting at your desk trying to send an email.

The Gut-Brain Axis – Mind Your Microbiome

Now, let's talk about something you might not expect: your gut. Yes, that's right, your gut and brain are BFFs, constantly communicating through what's called the "gut-brain axis." The idea is that what happens in your gut can actually affect how your brain works, and vice versa.

Your gut is filled with trillions of bacteria that make up what's called your **microbiome** (fancy word for the community of tiny living organisms in your gut), and these bacteria play a big role in your mood and anxiety levels. So if your gut health is out of balance, it can make you more prone to anxiety. This is why sometimes when you're stressed, you might feel it in your stomach (like those "butterflies" or that uneasy feeling).

Then there's the **vagus nerve**, which acts like a communication highway between your gut and your brain. When your gut's not happy, it sends signals up to your brain, which can influence your mood and anxiety levels. So yeah, it turns out the phrase "trust your gut" has a little more meaning than we thought!

Understanding Your Stress Response – Finding the Patterns

Take a moment to reflect on how anxiety shows up in your body. Do you feel your heart rate speed up? Maybe your muscles tense, or you get that "pit in your stomach" feeling? Start to notice these patterns, because they're clues to how your body reacts to stress. Once you start noticing these physical symptoms, it's like finding a map that helps you understand your anxiety a bit more clearly.

And remember, it's totally okay if this all feels overwhelming. Anxiety is complex, and your body is just doing its best to keep you safe—even if it feels like it's overreacting sometimes. We're going to learn how to calm that alarm system down together.

Key Takeaways

- **Stress and Anxiety Work Hand-in-Hand**: Stress is the external stuff that happens to you; anxiety is your internal reaction to that stress.
- **Your Body Is Wired to Respond to Threats**: Your fight, flight, freeze, or fawn response is your body's way of protecting you, but it sometimes overreacts in situations that aren't actually dangerous.
- **Understanding Your Brain and Body Is Empowering**: The more you learn about how your body responds to stress, the more you can work with your anxiety, rather than letting it take the wheel.

So there you have it—a little window into the science of stress and anxiety. It's all about making sense of what's going on inside so that we can start taking steps to bring balance and calm back into your life. You're doing great, and I'm so glad you're here.

6

Getting Personal – Understanding Your Anxiety Triggers

We've covered what anxiety is and how it works in the body, but now it's time to make it *personal*. And I mean, let's really dig into what makes your anxiety tick. Because anxiety doesn't just pop up for no reason—it usually has a trigger, something that sets off that chain reaction in your brain and body.

But here's the thing: your triggers are *your* triggers. They're as unique as you are. What sends you into an anxiety spiral might not phase someone else at all, and vice versa. The good news? Once you identify those triggers, you can learn to navigate them more effectively, which is a huge step toward managing your anxiety.

What's Triggering You?

Alright, let's start with the basics: a "trigger" is anything that sets off your anxiety. It could be a specific situation, a person, a thought, or even a physical sensation. The thing about triggers is that they can be really obvious, like an upcoming presentation at work, or super sneaky, like a certain smell or sound that takes you back to a stressful memory without you even realizing it.

Triggers can fall into a few different categories:

- **Situational Triggers**: These are external circumstances or events that make you feel anxious. Think social situations, crowded spaces, job interviews, public speaking, or deadlines. Basically, anything that puts you in a position where you feel "on the spot" or like you have to perform.
- **Emotional Triggers**: Sometimes, emotions themselves can be triggering. Feelings of sadness, anger, guilt, or overwhelm can bring up anxiety, especially if they're tied to past experiences or unresolved issues. For example, feeling left out by friends might trigger memories of rejection, making your anxiety jump in to protect you from feeling that pain again.
- **Relational Triggers**: Ever feel anxious around certain people? Maybe it's a boss who's hard to please, a family member who has high expectations, or even someone who just reminds you of a past negative experience. Relationships are a biggie when it comes to anxiety triggers because we're wired for connection, and anything that feels like a threat to that connection can set off alarm bells.

Avoidance and Coping Patterns

Okay, so let's say you've noticed that certain things make you anxious—like going to parties, talking to your boss, or trying something new. What do you do? If you're like most people, you probably try to cope. And sometimes, that means avoiding the situation entirely. Which, in theory, makes sense—if something makes you anxious, wouldn't it be easier to just... not do it?

The thing is, avoidance actually makes anxiety stronger over time. Here's why: every time you avoid a trigger, you're sending a message to your brain that the situation is truly dangerous, which reinforces the anxiety. So, the next time you're faced with that situation, your brain remembers *"Last time we ran away, so let's do it again!"* It's like trying to get rid of a fear of heights by avoiding tall buildings—you're not giving your brain a chance to learn that it's actually safe.

And let's be honest, avoidance can show up in all kinds of sneaky ways:

- **Over-preparing**: If you're anxious about a work presentation, you might spend hours and hours rehearsing it to the point of exhaustion.
- **Procrastination**: On the flip side, you might avoid starting something altogether because just thinking about it makes you anxious.
- **Distraction**: When you feel that anxiety coming on, it's easy to reach for your phone, watch TV, or do *anything* else to take your mind off of it.

But while these coping mechanisms can bring temporary relief, they tend to keep anxiety going in the long run. The goal is to face your triggers with new strategies, which we'll dive into soon.

Mapping Out Your Triggers

It's time for some detective work. Grab a pen and paper (or open a note on your phone), and let's start identifying what sets off your anxiety. Remember, this is all about curiosity, not judgment. You're just gathering information about your experience.

Step 1: Identify Situational Triggers Think about your day-to-day life. What situations tend to bring up anxiety for you? Is it getting ready to leave the house? Sitting down to tackle your emails? Meeting new people? Write down anything that comes to mind, even if it seems small or silly.

Step 2: Reflect on Emotional Triggers What emotions tend to make you feel anxious? Is it sadness, feeling out of control, frustration, or guilt? Sometimes, we don't even realize that certain emotions are uncomfortable for us until we sit down and really think about it.

Step 3: Consider Relational Triggers Who are the people that tend to trigger your anxiety? This doesn't mean they're bad people—sometimes it's just about how we relate to others. Maybe it's a coworker who's always negative, a friend who tends to criticize, or a parent who has high expectations.

Step 4: Look for Patterns Once you've listed out your triggers, start looking for patterns. Do certain situations trigger the same kinds of thoughts? Are there common themes, like feeling judged, fearing failure, or worrying about losing control? These patterns are going to be key in helping you figure out where to focus your energy as you start managing anxiety.

An Example – A Day in the Life of Triggers

To bring this to life, let's walk through a scenario. Let's say you're an office worker named Jamie. Here's how a typical day might play out with anxiety triggers:

- **Morning Routine**: Jamie wakes up and immediately feels a rush of anxiety. Why? Because mornings are a whirlwind of "I need to get ready," "What if I'm late?" and "I have so much to do today." Situational trigger: rushing around, feeling pressure.
- **The Commute**: On the way to work, Jamie's anxiety spikes while sitting in traffic. The thoughts start racing: *"I'm going to be late. My boss is going to think I'm irresponsible."* Relational trigger: worry about disappointing the boss.
- **Work Presentation**: Once at work, Jamie realizes there's a team meeting where they'll have to present an update. The anxiety ramps up again: *"What if I mess up? What if they ask a question I can't answer?"* Situational trigger: public speaking, fear of judgment.
- **After-Work Social**: A coworker invites Jamie out for drinks after work. Cue the anxiety thoughts: *"What if it's awkward? What if I don't have anything to say?"* Relational trigger:

social interactions, fear of embarrassment.

Notice how in each situation, Jamie's anxiety shows up in a different way. And for every anxious thought, there's a trigger behind it.

Reflecting on Your Own Triggers

Take some time to think about how these examples relate to you. Are there any situations or emotions that seem to push your anxiety buttons? And how do you tend to respond—do you avoid, over-prepare, or try to distract yourself?

Remember, there's no right or wrong way to experience anxiety. The whole point is to gain some self-awareness and figure out what makes your anxiety tick. Because once you know what your triggers are, you can start taking steps to face them in a healthier way.

Key Takeaways

- **Triggers Are Personal**: Your anxiety is unique to you, and so are your triggers. Whether it's a certain person, situation, or emotion, recognizing what sets off your anxiety is the first step to managing it.
- **Avoidance Is a Temporary Fix**: While it might feel good to avoid anxiety triggers in the short term, avoidance tends to reinforce anxiety over time.
- **Mapping Your Triggers Brings Awareness**: By reflecting

on your triggers, you gain insight into what's causing your anxiety and how to respond to it better.

So grab that pen and paper (or phone note) and start jotting down what comes to mind. The more you understand your anxiety, the more power you have to change your relationship with it. You've got this, and I'm right here with you.

7

The Mind's Playground – Unpacking Your Anxious Thoughts

So you've started to pinpoint some triggers—awesome work! But here's the next piece of the puzzle: how do your thoughts come into play when anxiety shows up? Because if you've ever felt like your mind is working against you—running wild with "what if" scenarios and spiraling thoughts—you're not alone. The truth is, anxiety loves to play in your mind, turning every situation into a playground for worries, doubts, and fears.

But just like with any playground, it's important to understand what's happening so you can take back control and navigate it with ease. In this chapter, we'll dig into how anxious thoughts take shape, the mental traps they set, and how you can challenge and reframe them to make your inner world a calmer place.

The Anxious Mindset – Where Do These Thoughts Come From?

Let's get one thing straight: your thoughts aren't "wrong" or "bad"—they're just your brain's way of trying to make sense of things. Anxiety is sneaky; it likes to weave its way into your thinking patterns without you even noticing. It's like a DJ in your head that keeps playing the same nervous song on repeat. Before you know it, your mind is stuck on that track, and it feels like there's no way to turn it off.

So where do these anxious thoughts come from? It usually starts with a trigger—a situation, feeling, or person that brings up anxiety. Then, your brain starts to play the "What if?" game:

- *"What if I mess up?"*
- *"What if they don't like me?"*
- *"What if something bad happens?"*

This "What if?" thinking is anxiety's favorite game, and it can be hard to win because it keeps your mind spinning with all the potential "bad" outcomes. But here's the thing: most of the time, those outcomes never happen. Yet your brain spends so much time and energy preparing for them that it feels like they're right around the corner.

The Cycle of Worry – How Anxious Thoughts Escalate

It usually goes something like this: you have a thought—say, *"What if I don't do well on this project?"*—and that thought creates a feeling, like fear or dread. That feeling then creates another thought, *"If I don't do well, my boss will be disappointed,"* and that thought creates even more anxiety. And on it goes, like a snowball rolling down a hill, getting bigger and bigger with every turn.

This is called a "thought-feeling loop," and it's a cycle that can be hard to break. The more you worry about something, the more anxious you feel, and the more anxious you feel, the more you worry. It's like being on a mental hamster wheel that just keeps spinning.

Common Thinking Traps – The Patterns of Anxious Thoughts

Anxiety has a way of distorting how you see the world, leading to thought patterns that make situations seem scarier than they really are. These are called "cognitive distortions" or "thinking traps," and they're like funhouse mirrors—they take something small and stretch or twist it until it looks way bigger or more distorted than it is.

Let's break down a few of the most common thinking traps so you can start to notice if they're showing up in your thought patterns:

Catastrophizing

This is when your brain goes straight to the worst-case scenario. It's like having a crystal ball that only shows doom and gloom. For example, if you're running late for a meeting, your thoughts might jump to, *"I'm going to get fired for being late, and then I won't be able to pay my bills, and then I'll lose my home."* It escalates quickly, turning a small issue into a giant crisis.

Overgeneralization

Ever have one bad experience and then think it's going to happen again and again? That's overgeneralization. For example, if you fail a test, you might think, *"I'm never going to pass any test— I'm just not smart enough."* It's taking one negative event and applying it to your entire life, which isn't fair to yourself or the situation.

Mind-Reading

This is when you assume you know what other people are thinking—and it's almost never good. *"She didn't text me back right away; she must be mad at me." "My coworker didn't say hi this morning; he probably thinks I'm incompetent."* The truth is, you can't actually read minds (no matter how much your anxiety tells you otherwise), and jumping to conclusions only makes you feel worse.

"Should" Statements

Be careful with those "should" thoughts—they can be sneaky. *"I should be doing more." "I shouldn't feel this way."* These thoughts set up unrealistic expectations for yourself and can make you feel guilty or like you're constantly falling short. In reality, life is full of "coulds" and "maybes," and holding yourself to strict "shoulds" just adds pressure.

Riding the Wave of Worry – Notice Without Judging

So, what do you do when those anxious thoughts come flooding in? First things first: know that it's okay to have these thoughts. Trying to "fight" anxiety only makes it fight back harder, so the key is to notice your thoughts without judging them.

Imagine your thoughts like waves in the ocean—some are big, some are small, and they're always coming and going. You don't have to dive into every wave that comes your way. Instead, you can ride them, let them pass, and choose which ones to pay attention to.

Here's a little exercise to help you practice:

1. **Label Your Thoughts**: When an anxious thought pops up, label it for what it is: *"That's a worry thought,"* or *"That's a mind-reading thought."* By naming it, you create a little bit of distance between you and the thought, which makes it easier to handle.

2. **Don't Judge**: Remind yourself that having anxious thoughts is normal—it's just your brain trying to protect

you. Instead of judging the thought, just notice it like you would notice a passing car: *"Oh, there goes a worry about my performance."*

3. **Focus on the Present**: Bring yourself back to the here and now. Anxiety tends to pull your mind into the future or the past, but right here, in this moment, you are safe. Notice your breath, feel your feet on the ground, and let the anxious thoughts float on by.

Challenging the "What Ifs" – Reframing Anxious Thoughts

Anxiety's favorite game is "What if?"—but you don't have to play along. One of the best ways to manage anxious thoughts is to challenge and reframe them. This means questioning the thought and coming up with a more balanced perspective.

Here's how to do it:

- **Catch the Thought**: Whenever you notice an anxious thought, like, *"What if I fail at this?"* write it down. Getting it out of your head and onto paper helps you see it more clearly.
- **Challenge the Thought**: Ask yourself: *"Is this thought 100% true? What evidence do I have for and against it? What would I say to a friend who was thinking this way?"* Often, you'll find that your anxious thoughts aren't as solid as they seem.
- **Reframe the Thought**: Once you've challenged the thought, come up with a more balanced or realistic way of looking at the situation. For example, if your thought is, *"I'm going*

to mess everything up," your reframe might be, *"It's okay if things don't go perfectly—I can handle whatever comes my way."*

Example of Reframing: Let's say you're about to start a new job, and your anxiety says, *"What if I'm not good enough? What if they made a mistake hiring me?"* Here's how you might challenge and reframe that:

- Challenge: *"I've been hired because they see my potential. I've succeeded in other jobs before, and I can learn and grow here, too."*
- Reframe: *"It's normal to feel nervous about something new, but I'm capable of figuring it out as I go."*

Reflect on Your Thinking Patterns

Take some time to reflect on which thinking traps resonate with you. Do you tend to catastrophize? Overgeneralize? Play the "What if?" game? Recognizing these patterns is a powerful step toward managing your anxiety because once you're aware of them, you can start to challenge them.

Remember, the goal isn't to stop having anxious thoughts altogether—that's not realistic (and wouldn't be all that helpful). The goal is to change your relationship with those thoughts, so they don't have as much power over you.

Key Takeaways

- **Anxiety Loves "What Ifs"**: Anxious thoughts tend to spiral and escalate, but you don't have to go along for the ride.
- **Watch Out for Thinking Traps**: Notice if you fall into patterns like catastrophizing, mind-reading, or "should" statements—they can make anxiety feel bigger than it is.
- **Challenge and Reframe**: Question your anxious thoughts and come up with more balanced, realistic thoughts, seeing them in a new light is a powerful way to reduce their impact and bring peace back into your mind.

Remember, you have the power to change your relationship with anxiety—one thought at a time. You're doing great, and I'm proud of you for taking these steps.

A Quick Request – Share Your Thoughts!

If you're finding this ebook helpful, I would be so grateful if you could leave a quick review on Amazon. Reviews are a powerful way to support both me as the author and future readers who can benefit from the tools and insights shared here. If you'd like to leave a review, here's how to do it:

1. **Head to the Amazon page** for this book. You can find it through your Amazon account by searching for the book title or visiting your purchase history.
2. **Scroll down to the review section**, where it says "Customer Reviews."
3. **Click on the "Write a customer review" button**, and share your thoughts! Whether it's a sentence or a paragraph, every bit helps.

Your review not only helps others discover the book but also provides them with the encouragement they might need to start their own journey of mastering anxiety. Thank you so much for being a part of this community and helping others find their path to peace!

8

Calming the Storm – Techniques to Soothe Anxiety in the Moment

When anxiety hits, it can feel like being caught in a storm—your heart races, your breath shortens, and it feels like there's nowhere to hide. In these moments, it can be hard to remember that you actually *have* tools to calm the storm, ground yourself, and find that stillness within. The good news is, you do!

This chapter is all about practical techniques you can use to bring yourself back to the present moment when anxiety shows up uninvited. Whether it's deep breathing, mindfulness, or creating a comforting environment, you'll learn strategies to help bring calm when anxiety tries to take the wheel.

Breath and Body-Based Techniques

One of the quickest ways to calm your anxiety is through your breath. Think of it like an anchor—when your mind is racing, and your thoughts feel like they're all over the place, your breath is something you can come back to that's steady, constant, and always available.

Here are a few breath–based techniques to try:

4-7-8 Breathing

This technique is super simple, but it's like a secret weapon for calming the nervous system. Here's how you do it:

1. Inhale quietly through your nose to a count of 4.
2. Hold your breath for a count of 7.
3. Exhale completely through your mouth to a count of 8.

Repeat this cycle a few times. This kind of slow, controlled breathing helps signal to your brain that you're safe and that it's okay to relax. It's almost like telling your body, *"Hey, it's all good—we can chill now."*

Box Breathing (4x4x4x4)

This is another great technique for anxiety because it focuses your mind and regulates your breathing all at once. Here's how you do it:

1. Inhale through your nose for a count of 4.
2. Hold your breath for a count of 4.
3. Exhale slowly through your mouth for a count of 4.
4. Hold your breath for another count of 4.

Picture drawing a box in your mind as you breathe in this pattern, going around the corners—inhale, hold, exhale, hold. Repeat this for a few minutes, and you'll start to notice a sense of calm wash over you.

Grounding Techniques to Bring You Back to the Present

When anxiety hits, it often pulls you out of the present moment—your thoughts jump to what *might* happen or what *has* happened. Grounding techniques are all about bringing you back to the here and now. They remind you that in this exact moment, you are safe, and you have control.

The 5-4-3-2-1 Grounding Exercise

This exercise uses your five senses to help you get back to the present:

- **5**: Acknowledge 5 things you can see around you. It could be anything—the trees outside, the coffee mug on your desk, the book on the shelf.
- **4**: Notice 4 things you can physically feel. The feeling of your feet on the floor, the texture of your clothing, the warmth of your coffee mug.
- **3**: Identify 3 things you can hear. Maybe it's birds chirping outside, the hum of your fridge, or the distant sound of cars.
- **2**: Notice 2 things you can smell. This might be tough in the moment, but if you can't smell anything, think of 2 scents you love.
- **1**: Focus on 1 thing you can taste. This could be as simple as noticing the taste in your mouth or taking a sip of water and

savoring it.

By engaging all your senses, this exercise grounds you in the present moment and pulls your mind away from the anxious thoughts.

Progressive Muscle Relaxation

This technique is perfect for letting go of tension in your body, which often builds up when you're anxious. Here's how you do it:

1. Start at your feet. Take a deep breath, tense your muscles (not too much), hold for a few seconds, and then release while exhaling.
2. Move up to your calves, thighs, stomach, hands, arms, shoulders, and so on—all the way to your head.
3. As you tense and relax each muscle group, notice how your body starts to relax more and more. It's like letting go of tiny anchors that have been keeping you stuck in anxiety.

This can be especially helpful before bed, or anytime you need to release physical tension.

Mindfulness and Meditation

Mindfulness is all about being present in the here and now—without judging your thoughts, feelings, or sensations. Easier said than done, right? The great thing is, it doesn't have to be complicated. And meditation is simply the practice of bringing mindfulness into your life.

Body Scan Meditation

The body scan is a simple mindfulness practice that brings awareness to each part of your body, helping you reconnect and find peace. Here's how:

1. Find a comfortable position, either sitting or lying down.
2. Close your eyes and take a few deep breaths, letting your body relax.
3. Start at the top of your head and slowly scan down your body, paying attention to how each part feels—without judgment. Notice any tension, warmth, tingling, or sensations that might be present.
4. Continue to slowly move your attention down your face, neck, shoulders, arms, chest, back, belly, hips, legs, and finally your feet. Just notice what's there.

This practice helps pull you away from anxious thoughts and into the experience of being in your body, which is often much calmer than being stuck in your head.

Mindful Breathing

It's as simple as it sounds: focusing your attention on your breath as it goes in and out of your body. Notice the rise and fall of your chest, the air filling your lungs, and the sensation of your breath moving in and out. When your mind wanders (because it will—it's what minds do), gently bring your attention back to the breath without judgment.

Mindful breathing is like a mini-meditation you can do anytime, anywhere. It brings you back to the present moment and helps you ride out the storm of anxiety.

Creating a Calm Space – Using Your Environment

Sometimes anxiety can feel like a storm brewing inside, and the best way to calm it down is to create a safe, peaceful space around you. Your environment can have a huge impact on how you feel, so finding ways to make it more comforting can make a big difference.

Here's how to create a calm space:

- **Declutter**: A cluttered space often leads to a cluttered mind. Take a few minutes to tidy up your space—it's amazing what a difference it can make in how you feel.
- **Use Calming Scents**: Scents like lavender, chamomile, and eucalyptus are known for their calming effects. Use a diffuser, scented candles, or essential oils to create a soothing aroma in your space.
- **Add Comforting Textures**: Think soft blankets, cozy pillows, or even a warm cup of tea in your hands. Engaging your sense of touch in a comforting way helps signal to your brain that it's safe to relax.
- **Play Relaxing Sounds**: Whether it's calming music, nature sounds, or white noise, adding auditory comfort to your space can help drown out the noise of anxious thoughts.

Your environment should be a space where you can find peace

and comfort, so don't be afraid to make it your own safe haven.

Reflect on What Works for You

The most important thing to remember is that not every technique will work for everyone. And that's okay! The goal is to find what feels good for *you* and use those tools whenever anxiety comes knocking. Maybe it's deep breathing before a big meeting, a quick body scan before bed, or lighting a candle while you journal out your thoughts. Whatever it is, know that these small moments of calm add up to a big impact on your overall well-being.

Key Takeaways

- **Breathe to Calm the Storm**: Simple breathwork exercises like 4-7-8 breathing or box breathing can quickly bring down anxiety and create a sense of calm.
- **Ground Yourself in the Present**: Grounding techniques like the 5-4-3-2-1 exercise help bring you back to the moment and away from anxious thoughts.
- **Create Your Safe Space**: Surround yourself with comforting textures, scents, and sounds that help soothe your senses and signal safety to your brain.

Remember, you don't need to do everything all at once—try one or two techniques that resonate with you, and see how they feel. You're building a toolkit to calm your mind and body, and every small step forward is something to be proud of.

9

Developing a Healthy Relationship with Anxiety

So far, we've talked about what anxiety is, where it comes from, and how it shows up in your body and mind. You've learned how to spot your triggers, understand your thought patterns, and practice techniques to bring yourself back to the present moment. But here's where we take it one step further: what if, instead of trying to get rid of anxiety, you learned to make peace with it?

I know that might sound like a big ask. After all, anxiety can feel like a bully that makes life more stressful. But imagine what would happen if you saw anxiety as a well-meaning but misguided friend—one that sometimes overreacts, but is ultimately just trying to keep you safe.

This chapter is all about developing a healthier, more compassionate relationship with your anxiety. It's not about pretending anxiety doesn't exist; it's about learning to understand, accept, and respond to it in a way that brings peace rather than conflict.

It's Okay to Feel Anxious

First things first: it's okay to feel anxious. Take a breath and let that sink in. You're not broken or "less than" for experiencing anxiety—it's a normal part of being human. In fact, it's part of what makes you a complex, emotionally rich person.

For a lot of people, the goal is to "get rid" of anxiety altogether, but that's not really how it works. Anxiety is part of your brain's natural survival system, and it's not going anywhere (and it actually plays a role in keeping you alert and safe). The trick is to work with it, not against it.

Think of it this way: if you were in a tug-of-war with your anxiety, constantly trying to pull it away, it would only pull harder. But what if you dropped the rope? You might find that without the struggle, anxiety becomes easier to understand and manage.

Self-Compassion – The Game Changer

When anxiety shows up, your first instinct might be to criticize yourself: *"Why am I like this? I shouldn't feel this way."* But beating yourself up only makes anxiety feel worse. Imagine telling a friend who's struggling, *"You're doing a terrible job at this, and you should be ashamed."* It wouldn't help them feel better—it would make them feel even more isolated and stuck.

Instead, try talking to yourself like you would to a friend—with kindness, understanding, and compassion. It might sound something like this:

- *"Hey, I know this is tough, but you're doing your best, and that's enough."*
- *"It's okay to feel what you're feeling. I'm here for you."*

Self-compassion is a game changer because it shifts the way you relate to your anxiety. Instead of seeing it as a sign that something's "wrong" with you, you start to see it as a part of yourself that needs care and attention.

The Power of Acceptance – Letting Go of the Struggle

One of the most powerful things you can do when dealing with anxiety is to practice acceptance. And no, I don't mean "giving in" to anxiety or letting it control your life. I mean accepting that anxiety is something you experience and giving yourself permission to feel it without fighting against it.

Here's an analogy: Imagine anxiety as a wave in the ocean. When you fight against the wave—trying to push it back or stop it from coming—it only knocks you over and pulls you under. But if you accept the wave, riding it out and letting it pass, you'll find that it's much easier to handle.

The same goes for anxiety. When you accept that it's there, rather than trying to "fix" it or push it away, you're able to experience it without getting swept away by it.

Mindful Acceptance in Practice

The next time anxiety shows up, take a moment to notice it without trying to change it. You might say to yourself, *"I'm noticing that I'm feeling anxious right now, and that's okay."* Breathe into the experience without judgment, and allow the feeling to be there.

It's like opening the door to an old friend who might overstay their welcome but is part of your life. You don't have to love that anxiety is there, but by accepting its presence, you take away its power.

Your Relationship with Anxiety – What Does It Look Like?

Take a moment to reflect on your relationship with anxiety. If anxiety were a person, how would you describe them? Are they like that friend who calls you all the time to make sure you're okay? Or maybe they're more like a strict teacher who's always worried you're going to get in trouble. How do you respond to them—are you annoyed, frustrated, or trying to ignore them altogether?

Once you've identified what your relationship with anxiety looks like, ask yourself: *"What kind of relationship do I want to have with it?"* Maybe you want to be more understanding, more compassionate, or less reactive. Whatever it is, know that it's possible to change your relationship with anxiety in a way that brings more peace to your life.

Embracing Your Authentic Self – You Are More Than Your Anxiety

Here's the truth: you are so much more than your anxiety. It's easy to start thinking of yourself as "an anxious person," but that's just one small part of who you are. You're also creative, caring, funny, determined, strong, and so much more. Your anxiety is just one thread in the rich tapestry of your life.

So when anxiety shows up, remember that it doesn't define you. It's a part of your experience, but it's not *who you are*. And by learning to understand and make peace with it, you can start living a life that feels more authentic and full—anxiety and all.

Learning to Befriend Your Anxiety

It might sound strange to think about befriending your anxiety, but hear me out. Anxiety is often just trying to help, even if it goes about it in a clumsy way. It's like a friend who shows up unannounced with good intentions but makes a bit of a mess.

So the next time anxiety knocks on your door, try greeting it with a little compassion and curiosity:

- *"Oh, hey anxiety. What's going on? What are you trying to protect me from right now?"*
- *"I see you're here again. Thanks for looking out for me—I know you're just trying to help, even if I don't need it right now."*

By taking this approach, you can start to build a healthier, more understanding relationship with anxiety—one that gives it space without letting it take over.

Key Takeaways

- **It's Okay to Feel Anxious**: Anxiety is a natural part of being human, and you don't need to criticize yourself for feeling it.
- **Practice Self-Compassion**: Talk to yourself like you would a friend who's struggling, offering kindness and understanding.
- **Accept Rather Than Fight**: The more you accept anxiety's presence, the less power it has to control your thoughts and actions.
- **Build a Healthy Relationship**: View anxiety as a part of yourself to care for, not something to fight against or get rid of.

You're on this journey to build a healthier relationship with anxiety, and each step you take brings you closer to peace and self-acceptance. Keep going—you're doing incredible work.

10

Building Resilience – Long-Term Strategies for Managing Anxiety

At this point, you've probably realized that dealing with anxiety isn't a one-time fix—it's a journey. And like any journey, you'll need to develop tools and habits that support you along the way. You've already learned how to calm anxiety in the moment, build a healthier relationship with it, and recognize your triggers and thought patterns. But now it's time to look at the bigger picture: how do you build long-term resilience so that anxiety has less power over your life in the future?

This chapter is all about creating a lifestyle that supports your mental health. We're going to dive into daily habits, mindful routines, and strategies for building emotional and physical resilience that make you stronger in the face of stress. Think of it as building a toolkit that will help you handle whatever comes your way.

Lifestyle Choices That Support Resilience

Anxiety doesn't just exist in your mind—it's connected to your body, your habits, and your environment. So, let's talk about some lifestyle changes that can help reduce anxiety and build up your mental resilience. Remember, these aren't "quick fixes," but rather long-term strategies that can make a big difference over time.

Exercise and Movement

Moving your body is one of the best things you can do to manage anxiety, and no—you don't have to become a marathon runner to feel the benefits. Whether it's a daily walk, a yoga session, or dancing around your living room to your favorite songs, exercise helps release endorphins (those feel-good chemicals) and reduces stress hormones like cortisol.

And don't worry about making it perfect. The goal isn't to have a rigid workout routine—it's to find something you enjoy that gets your body moving. Think of it like giving your anxiety a healthy outlet. Stressed? Take a walk. Feeling tense? Stretch it out. Find the kind of movement that feels good for *you*.

Balanced Nutrition

Ever notice how your mood changes when you're hungry? What you eat has a big impact on your anxiety levels, and eating balanced meals can help stabilize your blood sugar and your mood. Aim for a mix of protein, healthy fats, and complex carbs (like whole grains, fruits, and veggies). Foods rich in Omega-

3s (like salmon, walnuts, and chia seeds) and magnesium (like spinach, almonds, and dark chocolate) are known to support brain health and help regulate mood.

Also, try not to skip meals, and avoid too much caffeine or sugar—they might give you a quick energy boost, but they can also lead to crashes that make anxiety worse. Your brain and body need the right fuel to feel their best.

Quality Sleep

Let's talk about sleep—a huge factor when it comes to anxiety. If you're not getting enough rest, your body and mind don't have the chance to recharge, which can leave you feeling more anxious and irritable. Aim for 7-9 hours of quality sleep a night, and if you're struggling to get there, try creating a calming bedtime routine.

- **Wind Down Before Bed**: Dim the lights, put your phone away, and engage in calming activities like reading, taking a warm bath, or listening to soft music.
- **Stick to a Schedule**: Go to bed and wake up at the same time every day—even on weekends. This helps regulate your body's natural sleep-wake cycle.
- **Create a Comfortable Sleep Space**: Make sure your room is dark, cool, and quiet. Comfortable pillows, blankets, and even a white noise machine can make your sleep environment feel like a cozy cocoon.

Mindful Routines and Healthy Habits

Building resilience isn't just about "doing" things—it's also about *being* present, mindful, and intentional in your daily life. Small habits can have a big impact on how you experience anxiety, and integrating mindfulness into your routine can help you feel more balanced and grounded.

Daily Mindfulness Practice

Mindfulness doesn't have to mean sitting cross-legged on a cushion for hours (unless that's your thing!). It simply means paying attention to the present moment with curiosity and without judgment. And you can practice mindfulness in all kinds of ways: mindful eating, mindful walking, or simply noticing your breath throughout the day.

A simple way to start is to set aside just 5 minutes in the morning to sit quietly and focus on your breath. When your mind wanders (because it will), gently bring your attention back to your breath. Over time, this practice can help you build the mental muscles to stay present, even when anxiety tries to pull you away.

Gratitude Journaling

Gratitude has a powerful effect on your brain—it shifts your focus from what's "wrong" to what's going *right*. Every day, write down 3 things you're grateful for. They don't have to be big things; it could be the smell of your morning coffee, a hug from a friend, or even just a moment of peace. The act of noticing and appreciating the positives in your life can help balance out anxiety and bring a little more joy to your day.

Regular Relaxation Time

You don't have to "earn" relaxation—it's an essential part of your well-being. Make sure you're setting aside regular time to relax and do things that bring you joy. It could be reading a book, watching a funny show, taking a bath, or spending time in nature. Relaxation isn't a luxury; it's a necessity for managing anxiety and building resilience.

Building a Support Network – You Don't Have to Go It Alone

Anxiety loves to make you feel like you're alone, but the truth is, you're not. One of the most powerful ways to build resilience is to lean on the people around you. We're social creatures, and having a support system can help you manage anxiety and feel more connected.

Talk About It

Sometimes the hardest part is saying, *"Hey, I'm struggling."* But opening up to a trusted friend, family member, or therapist can be incredibly freeing. You don't have to share everything all at once—start small if that feels more comfortable. Just knowing that someone else understands what you're going through can make a world of difference.

Find Your Tribe

Find a community of people who "get" what you're going through. Whether it's a support group, an online community, or a circle of friends who share similar interests, being around people who are compassionate and understanding can help you feel less alone in your journey.

Professional Help is Always an Option

If anxiety is impacting your daily life and feels too big to handle on your own, it's okay to seek help. Therapy, coaching, and counseling are all ways to get support and learn additional tools for managing anxiety. Sometimes having someone to guide you can be the turning point you need.

Reflect on What Resilience Looks Like for You

The most important thing to remember is that resilience isn't about being perfect or never feeling anxious again. It's about learning to take care of yourself, build habits that support your well-being, and find ways to bounce back when anxiety shows up. And resilience looks different for everyone—it's about what feels supportive for *you*.

Take a moment to think about which of these strategies resonate with you. What's one small change you can make today to build your resilience? It doesn't have to be big—even the smallest step forward is a victory.

Key Takeaways

- **Lifestyle Choices Matter**: Regular movement, balanced nutrition, and quality sleep are all important parts of managing anxiety and building resilience.
- **Mindful Habits Support Well-Being**: Daily mindfulness, gratitude journaling, and regular relaxation help balance your mental health and reduce stress.
- **Build Your Support Network**: Don't be afraid to reach out to friends, family, or a professional when anxiety feels overwhelming. Connection and support are key to resilience.

Remember, building resilience is a journey, not a destination. Every mindful moment, healthy choice, and act of self-compassion adds up, making you stronger and more equipped to handle whatever life throws your way. You're on the right path, and I'm proud of you for taking these steps.

11

The Role of Humor and Light-Heartedness in Managing Anxiety

Anxiety can make everything feel so... heavy. When you're caught in an anxious thought spiral, it can seem like there's no way to find lightness or relief. But here's a little secret that's helped so many people, time and time again: humor is one of the most powerful ways to break anxiety's grip. Laughing, finding joy in the little things, and approaching life with a sense of playfulness can make the tough stuff feel a whole lot easier.

In this chapter, we're going to talk about the power of humor and how it can be a surprising (and effective) tool in managing anxiety. You'll learn how to use laughter as a stress reliever, find light-hearted moments in everyday life, and start seeing things in a way that's a little more playful and a lot less serious.

Laughter as a Stress Reliever – Why Humor Matters

Let's start with a simple truth: laughter feels good. Think about the last time you had a real, deep belly laugh—the kind that makes your eyes water and your stomach hurt. For that moment, whatever was on your mind seemed to fade away, and all that mattered was the joy of the moment. That's the power of laughter.

But there's actually science behind why humor is such a great stress reliever. When you laugh, your brain releases endorphins (those feel-good chemicals) and reduces the levels of cortisol (the stress hormone). It's like hitting a "reset" button on your mood. And laughter isn't just a mental thing—it has physical benefits too. It relaxes your muscles, lowers your blood pressure, and even boosts your immune system.

The best part? You don't have to wait for a funny moment to "happen" to you. You can actively seek out laughter and humor in your everyday life.

Finding Humor in Everyday Situations

One of the best ways to manage anxiety is to find the humor in your situation—even when things don't seem all that funny. Now, I'm not saying you have to turn every stressful moment into a comedy show, but learning to see the lighter side of life can make a big difference.

Laugh at the Little Things

When you're feeling anxious, even small inconveniences can seem like big deals. But what if you tried to laugh at those little moments? Maybe you spilled your coffee all over your favorite shirt on the way to work—yes, it's frustrating, but it's also a little ridiculous when you think about it. Or maybe you trip over your own feet while walking down the street—sure, it's embarrassing, but you can laugh at yourself instead of getting caught up in feeling clumsy.

By laughing at the little things, you start to break the cycle of anxiety and remind yourself that not everything has to be so serious. And when you find joy in the awkward, the messy, and the unexpected, you'll find it's easier to let go of the stress.

Let Yourself Be Silly

When was the last time you did something just for fun, with no expectations or pressure? Anxiety loves to make everything feel like it's high-stakes, but sometimes the best way to shake that off is to let yourself be silly. Dance around the house to your favorite song, make goofy faces in the mirror, or play a game that you haven't played in years.

Silliness can feel like a relief, a way to break out of your head and connect with a more carefree part of yourself. It doesn't matter what you do—what matters is that you let yourself have fun without overthinking it.

The Benefits of a Playful Mindset

One of the most effective ways to counter anxiety is to adopt a playful mindset. This doesn't mean ignoring serious situations or pretending everything's okay when it's not—it means approaching life with curiosity, lightness, and the willingness to see the humor in things.

Reframe Anxiety as an Adventure

Imagine anxiety as a character in your life—a quirky sidekick who's always over-prepared and ready for the worst-case scenario. You could say, *"Oh, here comes Anxiety, packing an emergency kit for our trip to the grocery store."* By personifying your anxiety in a playful way, you take some of its power away and make it feel a little less intimidating.

Laugh at the "What Ifs"

Anxiety is full of "What if?" questions: *"What if I say something wrong?" "What if things don't go as planned?" "What if everyone hates me?"* These questions can feel serious and scary, but what if you responded to them with humor?

- *"What if I say something wrong?" "Well, then I guess I'll start a new trend for awkward conversations."*
- *"What if things don't go as planned?" "Maybe I'll discover something amazing in Plan B."*
- *"What if everyone hates me?" "Then I'll have lots of free time!"*

By laughing at the "What ifs," you stop giving them so much

weight. Humor becomes a way to let go of the pressure and see that even if things don't go perfectly, you can still find something to laugh about.

Creating Joyful Moments

Joy isn't something you have to wait for—it's something you can create, even on tough days. When anxiety feels heavy, finding small moments of joy can be a powerful way to bring light back into your life.

Make a "Joy List"

Take a few minutes to make a list of things that bring you joy. It can be anything—small or big, simple or elaborate. Maybe it's watching your favorite comedy, going for a walk in nature, calling a friend who always makes you laugh, or treating yourself to your favorite snack. Keep this list handy and refer to it whenever you need a little pick-me-up. You'll find that sometimes, even the smallest joy can be the thing that turns your day around.

Find Humor in Your Favorite Things

Actively seek out things that make you laugh. Watch funny videos, listen to stand-up comedy, read a book that makes you smile, or share a joke with a friend. The point is to fill your life with things that make you laugh and remind you that joy is always within reach.

Reflect on How Humor Fits Into Your Life

Take a moment to think about how humor shows up in your life. Do you find yourself laughing every day, or has it been a while since you've let yourself really have fun? What are some small, simple ways you can bring more humor and joy into your day-to-day life? Remember, it doesn't have to be anything grand—sometimes a good laugh is all it takes to break the tension and bring you back to the present.

You're allowed to find humor in the serious stuff, and you're allowed to laugh even when things aren't perfect. Because here's the truth: laughter is one of the best ways to find peace and lighten the load that anxiety puts on your shoulders.

Key Takeaways

- **Humor is a Powerful Tool**: Laughter releases feel-good chemicals, reduces stress hormones, and can change the way you experience anxiety.
- **Find Joy in the Everyday**: Let yourself laugh at the little things, be silly, and approach life with a playful mindset.
- **Create Moments of Joy**: Make a "joy list" of things that make you happy, and actively seek out humor in your favorite activities.

Remember, laughter is a tool that's always available to you, and joy is something you can create at any moment. So go ahead— let yourself laugh, find the humor in the chaos, and know that it's okay to lighten up and have fun.

12

Putting It All Together – Crafting Your Roadmap to Well-Being

Congratulations—you've made it to the final chapter! You've learned about what anxiety is, how it shows up in your mind and body, and practical strategies for both soothing it in the moment and building long-term resilience. Now it's time to put it all together into a plan that works for *you*. Think of this chapter as your blueprint for living a more balanced, peaceful life, where anxiety doesn't call the shots.

The truth is, learning to manage anxiety is an ongoing journey. It's not about achieving "perfection" or never feeling anxious again; it's about creating a life where anxiety doesn't hold you back, where you can live more freely, and where you have the tools to take care of yourself when things get tough. Let's put all the pieces together so you can create a roadmap that's as unique as you are.

Step 1: Know Your Triggers and Patterns

By now, you've probably identified a few things that tend to trigger your anxiety—whether it's social situations, work stress, or simply those "what if?" thoughts that pop up out of nowhere. Take some time to reflect on the patterns you've noticed in your journey through this book.

- **What are your most common triggers?** Are there specific situations, places, or people that tend to set off your anxiety?
- **How does anxiety show up for you?** Is it mostly physical (like a racing heart), mental (like spiraling thoughts), or a mix of both?
- **What are your coping habits?** Do you tend to avoid certain situations, overprepare, or try to distract yourself?

Understanding your triggers and patterns is like putting together a map of your anxiety. The more you know about how it operates, the easier it will be to manage it.

Step 2: Build Your Anxiety Toolkit

Throughout this book, we've explored a variety of tools and techniques for managing anxiety, from breathwork to grounding exercises to gratitude journaling. Now it's time to build your personalized "anxiety toolkit"—the collection of practices that work best for you.

Take a moment to think about which tools resonate with you. What techniques have felt the most helpful in calming your mind and body? Here are a few examples of tools you might include:

- **Breath-Based Tools**: 4-7-8 breathing, box breathing, mindful breathing
- **Grounding Techniques**: 5-4-3-2-1 sensory grounding, progressive muscle relaxation
- **Mindfulness Practices**: Body scan meditation, daily mindful moments
- **Journaling & Reflection**: Gratitude journaling, writing down anxious thoughts and reframing them
- **Joy & Laughter**: Activities that make you laugh, joyful moments from your "joy list"

Your anxiety toolkit is yours to create, and there's no right or wrong way to fill it. Try to have a variety of techniques that work for different situations—some tools might be great for when you're feeling anxious in the moment, while others might help you build long-term resilience.

Step 3: Make Self-Care Non-Negotiable

Self-care isn't just something "nice to have"—it's a critical part of managing anxiety and maintaining your well-being. Remember, self-care doesn't have to be elaborate. It's about small, everyday choices that support your mental, emotional, and physical health.

Here are some self-care habits to integrate into your routine:

- **Regular Movement**: Whether it's a walk, stretching, yoga, or dancing, moving your body helps regulate stress.

- **Quality Sleep**: Create a calming bedtime routine to ensure you get the rest your body and mind need.
- **Balanced Nutrition**: Nourish your body with balanced meals, and avoid too much caffeine or sugar that might trigger anxiety spikes.
- **Intentional Relaxation**: Schedule time for relaxation and joy—whether it's reading a book, spending time with loved ones, or just taking a moment to breathe.

Think of self-care as a way of filling your own cup so that you have the energy and strength to take on whatever comes your way. And remember, self-care is not selfish—it's necessary for living a balanced, healthy life.

Step 4: Build a Supportive Environment

One of the most powerful ways to manage anxiety is to create an environment that feels safe, supportive, and uplifting. This includes both your physical environment and your social connections.

Create a Calming Space

Your surroundings play a big role in how you feel, so take time to make your space feel like a sanctuary. Whether that means decluttering, adding plants, setting up a cozy corner for meditation, or playing calming music, your environment should support your well-being.

Nurture Positive Relationships

Surround yourself with people who uplift you, understand you, and make you feel supported. Anxiety loves to isolate, but you don't have to go through it alone. Build connections with friends, family, or supportive communities that help you feel understood and connected.

Ask for Help When Needed

Remember, it's okay to reach out for help when you need it— whether that's talking to a friend, seeking professional therapy, or joining a support group. Asking for help is a sign of strength, not weakness, and sometimes a little guidance can make all the difference in managing anxiety.

Step 5: Embrace Progress, Not Perfection

One of the most important things to remember is that this journey is about progress, not perfection. You're going to have days where anxiety feels more manageable, and days where it feels like a struggle—that's okay. It doesn't mean you're doing something wrong; it just means you're human.

Celebrate the small victories—whether it's using a grounding technique in a stressful situation, taking a moment to laugh at yourself, or simply showing up and doing your best. Every step forward, no matter how small, is a step toward greater well-being.

It's okay to be imperfect. It's okay to struggle. And it's okay to give yourself grace as you navigate the ups and downs of managing anxiety. Remember, you're building a relationship with yourself that's based on understanding, compassion, and support.

Your Personalized Roadmap – Putting It All Together

Take a moment to reflect on everything you've learned throughout this book. What tools and techniques stood out to you? What habits or routines do you want to integrate into your life? And how can you make self-care a non-negotiable part of your well-being?

This roadmap is yours to create, and it's going to look different for everyone. It's a journey of self-discovery, growth, and finding what works best for you. And as you continue to navigate your relationship with anxiety, know that you have everything you need within you to find peace, balance, and joy.

Key Takeaways

- **Understand Your Triggers and Patterns**: Reflect on what tends to trigger your anxiety and how it shows up for you.
- **Build Your Toolkit**: Create a collection of tools and techniques that help you calm anxiety and build resilience over time.
- **Prioritize Self-Care**: Make self-care a regular part of your life, focusing on movement, sleep, nutrition, and relaxation.

- **Create a Supportive Environment**: Surround yourself with calming spaces and uplifting people who support your well-being.
- **Embrace Progress Over Perfection**: Remember that managing anxiety is a journey, and every step forward is worth celebrating.

You've got this. You're doing the work, and that's something to be incredibly proud of. Take your time, be kind to yourself, and remember that this journey is all about finding what feels right for *you*. And wherever you are on this path, know that you're exactly where you need to be.

13

Thank You

Thank you for taking this journey with me. I know that diving deep into understanding and managing anxiety isn't always easy, but I truly hope that the tools, insights, and practices shared in this book have given you the support, understanding, and encouragement you need to navigate your own path. Remember, every step you take—no matter how small—is a victory worth celebrating.

Anxiety can feel overwhelming, but you're not alone in this. You have the power to change your relationship with anxiety, to live a life of greater peace, and to find joy even in the little moments. You've already taken such a powerful step by being here, and I'm so grateful that you've chosen to let me be a part of your journey.

If at any point you feel like you need further support—whether it's personalized coaching, consulting for your unique situation, or simply more guidance on integrating these practices into your life—please don't hesitate to reach out. You can find more resources, information on coaching or consulting, and additional support on my website www.somebodylikeyou.org, or feel free to send me an email at somebodylikeyou444@gmail.com.

Whatever your needs may be, know that I'm here to help you on your journey to greater mental well-being, balance, and fulfillment.

If you found this book helpful in your journey to mastering anxiety, I would be so grateful if you could take a moment to leave a review on Amazon. Your feedback not only supports me as an author but also helps future readers discover this book and benefit from its message. By sharing your experience, you're helping others find the guidance and support they need to navigate their own paths toward peace and well-being. It's a great way to give back and pay it forward to those who are also seeking to understand and manage their anxiety.

Thank you for being open, for showing up for yourself, and for taking these steps toward greater well-being. Keep going, keep growing, and remember: you are not defined by your anxiety. You are so much more—strong, capable, and deserving of a life filled with peace and joy.

With gratitude and all my support,

Ben Meyers

Founder, Somebody Like You Mental Health Services

Certified Integrative Mental Health Coach & Consultant

www.ingramcontent.com/pod-product-compliance
Lightning Source LLC
Chambersburg PA
CBHW061516250726
48657CB00005B/1894